Contents | Surf the Internet

W9-AOA-544

How to Use This Book

Each Step Back Science book traces the path of a science-based act backwards, from its result to its beginning.

Each double-page spread like the ones below explains one step in the process.

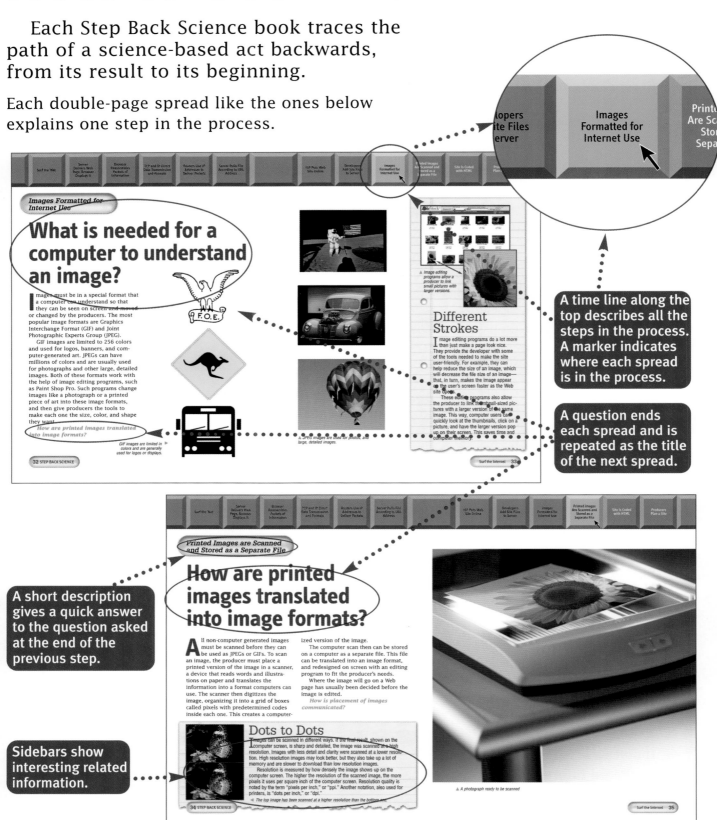

A time line along the top describes all the steps in the process. A marker indicates where each spread is in the process.

A question ends each spread and is repeated as the title of the next spread.

A short description gives a quick answer to the question asked at the end of the previous step.

Sidebars show interesting related information.

Images Formatted for Internet Use

What is needed for a computer to understand an image?

Images must be in a special format that a computer can understand so that they can be seen on screen and moved or changed by the producers. The most popular image formats are Graphics Interchange Format (GIF) and Joint Photographic Experts Group (JPEG).

GIF images are limited to 256 colors and used for logos, banners, and computer-generated art. JPEGs can have millions of colors and are usually used for photographs and other large, detailed images. Both of these formats work with the help of image editing programs, such as Paint Shop Pro. Such programs change images like a photograph or a printed piece of art into these image formats, and then give producers the tools to make each one the size, color, and shape they want.

How are printed images translated into image formats?

GIF images are limited in colors and are generally used for logos or displays.

JPEG images are used for photos and large, detailed images.

Different Strokes

Image editing programs do a lot more than just make a page look nice. They provide the developer with some of the tools needed to make the site user-friendly. For example, they can help reduce the size of an image, which will decrease the file size of an image—that, in turn, makes the image appear on the user's screen faster as the Web site opens.

These editing programs also allow the producer to link thumbnail-sized pictures with a larger version of the same image. This way, computer users can quickly look at the thumbnails, click on a picture, and have the larger version pop up on their screen. This saves time and computer memory.

Image editing programs allow a producer to link small pictures with larger versions.

Printed Images are Scanned and Stored as a Separate File

How are printed images translated into image formats?

All non-computer generated images must be scanned before they can be used as JPEGs or GIFs. To scan an image, the producer must place a printed version of the image in a scanner, a device that reads words and illustrations on paper and translates the information into a format computers can use. The scanner then digitizes the image, organizing it into a grid of boxes called pixels with predetermined codes inside each one. This creates a computerized version of the image.

The computer scan then can be stored on a computer as a separate file. This file can be translated into an image format, and redesigned on screen with an editing program to fit the producer's needs.

Where the image will go on a Web page has usually been decided before the image is edited.

How is placement of images communicated?

Dots to Dots

Images can be scanned in different ways. If the final result, shown on the computer screen, is sharp and detailed, the image was scanned at a high resolution. Images with less detail and clarity were scanned at a lower resolution. High resolution images may look better, but they also take up a lot of memory and are slower to download than low resolution images.

Resolution is measured by how densely the image shows up on the computer screen. The higher the resolution of the scanned image, the more pixels it uses per square inch of the computer screen. Resolution quality is noted by the term "pixels per inch," or "ppi." Another notation, also used for printers, is "dots per inch," or "dpi."

The top image has been scanned at a higher resolution than the bottom one.

A photograph ready to be scanned

Side Step spreads, like the one below, offer separate but related information.

The Big Picture, on pages 40–41, shows you the entire process at a glance.

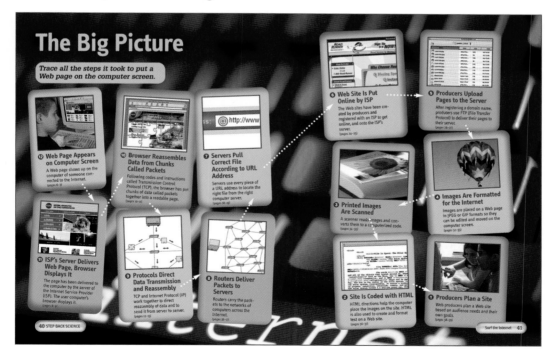

Surf the 'Net

How does the Internet work?

Now on your computer screen for your education or entertainment: a web page, brought to you by the Internet. The Internet contains trillions of words, images, sounds, and movies on thousands of subjects, brought to the convenience of your computer's screen through an enormous international network of computers, cables, and satellites.

By the time a web page appears on your screen, it has been through an amazing journey—all the more amazing because it only took seconds. But first things first:

What causes a web page to show up on your screen?

Surfing Hardware

You need a *computer* powered by electricity or a battery.

All computer viewing takes place on a *screen*.

The *mouse* lets the user move around a site's pages and click on highlighted links that open other web pages.

A *modem* is a device that lets you receive and transmit material over telephone lines or cables.

A *telephone or cable TV hook-up* connects the user's computer to a network of other computers through satellites in space that pick up signals from other computers.

Surfing Software

A *browser*, such as Microsoft Internet Explorer or Netscape Navigator, is a software program that locates and displays web pages on the Internet.

The *browser line*, or address line, is the space where you type a web address.

The *cursor* is a pointer that shows where the mouse is moving.

By clicking the mouse on the backward and forward *arrow buttons*, you can see previously viewed pages.

ISP Puts
Website On-Line

Developers
Add Site Files
to Server

Images
Formatted for
Internet Use

Printed Images
Are Scanned and
Stored as a
Separate File

Site Is Coded
with HTML

Producers
Plan a Site

arrow buttons

browser line

browser

cursor

monitor

screen

computer

mouse

modem

Server Delivers Web Page, Browser Displays It

What causes a web page to show up on your computer screen?

The page is displayed on screen by a program on your computer called a browser. The most popular browsers are Internet Explorer and Netscape Navigator. Before the browser can display the page, however, you must be connected to the Internet through an Internet Service Provider (ISP), such as Yahoo, Earthlink, AOL, Mindspring, or others. Think of ISPs as gateways to the Internet, and its managers as well. ISPs manage the process of requesting and retrieving information 24 hours a day—which is why you must generally pay a monthly fee for the service.

Your computer browser retrieves the web page from a server, a computer where web pages are stored. The pages are broken into chunks of data called packets.

What does your browser do with the packets?

It Pays to Advertise

Most Internet users are charged a monthly fee by their ISP, which offers a link to computer networks around the world in the form of a software package, user name, password, and access phone number. The ISP may also offer special "member-only" services, such as instant on-screen messaging among members. Since the creators of websites, also called developers, must also pay an ISP, many of them include product or service advertisements on the web pages you view. These ads are almost always "clickable," which means clicking on them will bring the user to the advertiser's linked web page. Advertisers may pay the website owner to place the ad and give additional money based on the number of "clicks" they get.

▲ *The home page of a website, like the table of contents of a book, offers a brief description of what is inside.*

Browser Reassembles Packets of Information

What does the browser do with the packets?

Like connecting pieces of a jigsaw puzzle, your browser puts the packets together into a unified page that will make sense when you view it on screen. Each packet, which can hold up to 1,500 letters, numbers, or symbols, travels separately, like individual pieces of mail arriving at the same mailbox. The packets may arrive out of order. They may be coming from different places, so some will arrive before others. Other packets may not have arrived at all. The browser checks the information in each packet and makes sure everything is complete. Then it puts all the packets together in their proper order.

The data in the packets, including the contents and the address information, is made of thousands and thousands of lines of a computer language called HTML, which stands for HyperText Mark-up Language. The server follows coded HTML instructions for how to display the page. It also follows something called Transmission Control Protocol (TCP).

What is Transmission Control Protocol?

Mode of Transportation

▲ *A modem*

The speed at which information can be sent over the Internet has a lot to do with the computer user's modem. A modem—short for modulator-demodulator—is a device that provides a way for a computer to transmit data over telephone or cable lines. It translates the information from digital numbers (as a computer would store it) to a form that can be transmitted over these lines (in invisible waves of electricity).

Nowadays most modems are built into the body of the computer. Others connect to the computer via a cable, or are offered as a card that can slide into a slot on the computer.

How fast the modem can transmit and receive data is measured in bps, or bits per second. Today the fastest modems run at 57,600 bps, but both the computer doing the sending and the one receiving would need these high-speed modems for the fastest possible exchange of data.

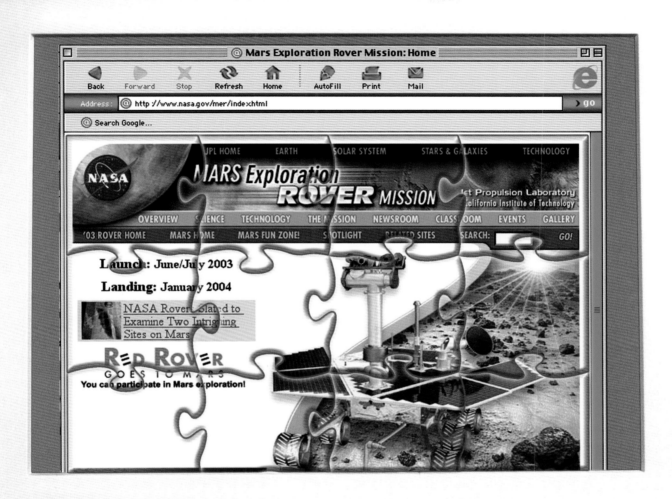

▲ *A computer browser assembles separated packets into a page that makes sense, like putting together a puzzle.*

TCP and IP Direct Data Transmission and Formats

What is Transmission Control Protocol?

Transmission Control Protocol (TCP) is one of two major sets of rules that govern every computer on the Internet. The other major protocol is Internet Protocol (IP). These two protocols have separate responsibilities, but they work together to link computers so data can be exchanged quickly and efficiently.

Before the web page reached your computer, it was in a server, which may have been thousands of miles away. Between the two computers are relay stations called routers. Routers link computers together into groups called networks.

The routers find the best routes, or passages, across their networks so the packets can quickly travel to their final destination (your computer.) TCP breaks files down into packets and IP directs the routing process. When the packets reach their destination, TCP reassembles them.

But how do routers choose the passages or routes?

Other Protocols

TCP/IP is the major protocol system on the Internet, but other protocols are at work too. SMTP—Simple Mail Transfer Protocol—works with e-mail. FTP—File Transfer Protocol—is needed for uploading and downloading files to and from other computers. HTTP in the browser line stands for HypterText Transfer Protocol. The protocols all help computers communicate with and understand each other.

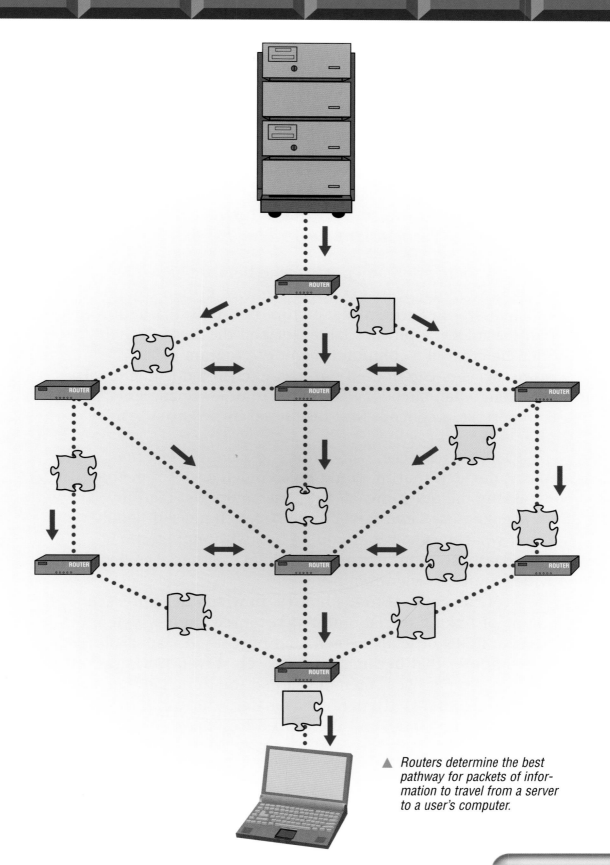

▲ Routers determine the best pathway for packets of information to travel from a server to a user's computer.

THINK BIG

How did a computer scientist named Tim Berners-Lee help shape the Internet?

Though there are many people who helped shape the World Wide Web, one of its key inventors was British computer scientist Tim Berners-Lee, pictured at right. In 1980, while working at CERN, a physics laboratory on the Swiss-French border, he created a computer memory program called Enquire. Berners-Lee figured out a way to fill a document with words that, when clicked, would lead to other documents. This was hypertext, a concept first discussed by scientist Vannevar Bush in 1945.

By 1989, Berners-Lee, who admits to having a terrible memory, decided that "it would be so much easier if everybody asking me questions all the time could just read my database (Enquire), and it would be so much nicer if I could find out what these guys are doing by just jumping into a similar database of information for them." Berners-Lee decided to widen Enquire's viewership.

He wrote a proposal to his bosses, in which he expressed the hope of linking the laboratory's resources to his system by hypertext. CERN officials agreed, and purchased a specially made computer that became the first web server. Working with colleagues, Berners-Lee then developed the three key tools of the web: HTML, HTTP (HyperText Transfer Protocol, the system for linking documents), and the URL addressing system.

You're in the Army Now

The Internet originated in 1969 as a network of military-oriented computer databases. The network, called ARPAnet (Advanced Research Projects Agency network), linked workers at the U.S. Department of Defense. In the 1970s, the information system was opened to universities and businesses doing defense-related research. Its audience grew throughout the 1980s as other schools and businesses learned about the information available through the computer network.

Routers Use IP Addresses to Deliver Packets

How do routers choose the passages or routes for the packets?

When a router receives a packet, it checks the packet's address. Each computer on the Internet has its own unique address, called an IP address. This is a series of four numbers or groups of numbers connected by dots.

The address can tell a lot about where the packet is going. By analyzing this number, the router can tell if the packet is going to a computer that is within the router's own network. If the router controls the computer that the packet is meant for, it delivers the packet directly to the computer. If the router doesn't control the target computer, it sends the packet to another router. This new router makes the same decision: deliver the packet, or pass it on? This process continues until the packet reaches its final destination: your computer.

But how does the server know which web page you wanted?

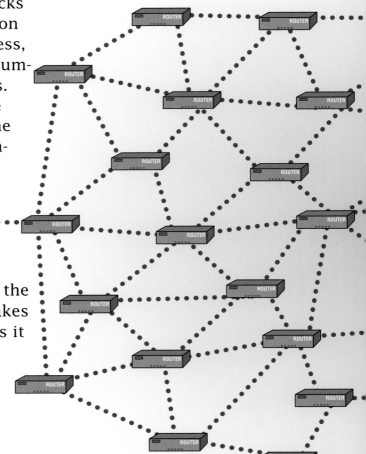

▲ *Satellites can make Internet data transmission even faster.*

Fast as It Can

Information travels over the Internet at lightning-fast speeds with the help of modern technology, including cable hook-ups and satellites. Satellites can bounce information in the form of electrical signals down to Earth an average of ten times faster than a traditional telephone line connection to the Internet.

With a satellite connection, requests are sent normally over telephone lines. However, instead of transferring information directly back to the user over the same phone line, the server sends the information to a satellite company's network operations center. From there, the information is directed to a satellite high above Earth. Within seconds, the information bounces down to a satellite dish in or near the user's home and reaches the user's PC through the same kind of cable used by cable TV systems.

▼ *Using a computer's IP address, routers carry packets of information through the Internet to their destination.*

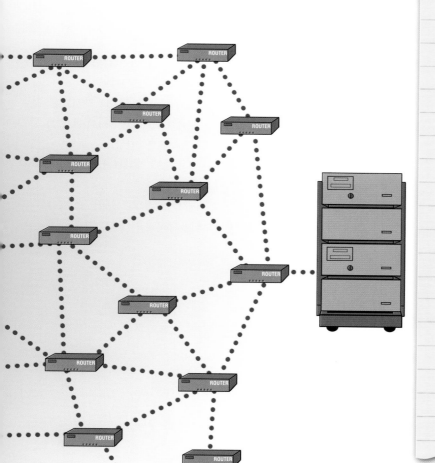

Server Pulls File According to URL Address

How does the server know which web page you wanted?

The server on the other side of all those networked routers pulled the file according to the address you typed into your browser line. That address, called a URL, contained all the information necessary to locate the right file, after which it was broken down into packets and sent to the right place, all according to TCP/IP.

URL stands for Uniform Resource Locator. It is used just like any other address: as a kind of a map to locate someone or something. URL addresses give each page on the web its own series of letters and symbols that represent it and make it a unique destination. No two sites have the same URL.

Each part of the address you typed is important. (See right.)

But how does a web page get onto a server in the first place?

Their Own Domain

The abbreviations used at the end of domain names (called top-level domains, or TLDs) are designed to help organize the Internet's domains into categories. Two-letter TLDs show the country in which the domain is registered (see page 43 for more). Other TLDs may tell you something about the domain's owner or its purpose. As the number of websites has grown, so has the list of top-level domains. Here are some common ones.

.com	commercial	.gov	government
.org	organization	.mil	military
.net	ISP or network	.info	information for the public
.edu	school		

The first part of the address tells your computer what it is about to do.

http *(HyperText Transfer Protocol) commands the computer to get ready to display a file posted somewhere on the World Wide Web.*

The slashes (//) prompt the computer to recognize that the full address of the file will follow.

The second part of the address identifies the specific computer that has the file you want to see. This other computer, which is connected to the Internet somewhere for the purpose of sharing files, functions as a server.

www *is the name of a server that belongs to nasa.gov. www is the traditional name for a domain's main web server.*

nasa.gov *is the site's domain name, and it identifies the organization that owns or rents the server. The "gov" part of the address shows that NASA is a government organization. (See page 43 for more on address suffixes.)*

@ http://www.nasa.gov/mer/index.html

The third part of the address identifies the exact file you want from the server you have identified.

/mer/ *tells the computer to search inside a directory (a group of files, like a folder) on the nasa.gov website with the name "mer," as in Mars Exploration Rover.*

index.html *tells the computer to get the file with the name "index.html" from inside the "mer" directory. Short for HyperText Markup Language,* **html** *indicates that the file contains the code that makes up a web page. Other endings indicate other kinds of files: .gif and .jpg, for example, are two kinds of picture files commonly used on the Internet.*

Back **Forward** **Stop** **Refresh** **Home** **AutoFill** **Print** **Mail**

Address: http://www.nasa.gov/mer/index.html

JPL HOME   EARTH   SOLAR SYSTEM   STARS & GALAXIES   TECHNOLOGY

NASA **MARS Exploration ROVER MISSION**   Jet Propulsion Laboratory California Institute of Technology

OVERVIEW   SCIENCE   TECHNOLOGY   THE MISSION   NEWSROOM   CLASSROOM   EVENTS   GALLERY

'03 ROVER HOME   MARS HOME   MARS FUN ZONE!   SPOTLIGHT   RELATED SITES   SEARCH: GO!

Launch: June/July 2003

Landing: January 2004

NASA Rovers Slated to Examine Two Intriguing Sites on Mars

RED ROVER GOES TO MARS You can participate in Mars exploration!

ATHENA INSTRUMENT SITE

CREDITS   FEEDBACK   NASA PRIVACY STATEMENT   SITEMAP

DESTINATION UNKNOWN

How do computer users search for information if they do not know the URL address?

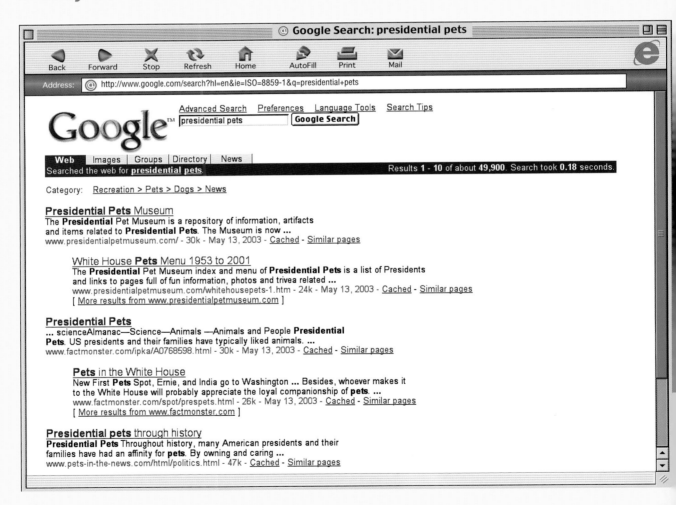

They can type in the address of an Internet search engine. Search engines are separate, privately owned websites that are programmed to analyze keywords typed in by the user and match them with keywords in its own database.

Here is how it works: You type in the URL address of a search engine, such as *Yahoo.com*, *Ask.com*, or *Google.com*. The site's home page will provide a space to type in keywords to help find the best websites. For example, if you are looking for information on presidential pets, type in "presidential pets" or "White House animals." If these keywords match those found in the search engine's database, the site will then show a screen providing URL addresses for specific websites. All of the highlighted or underlined sites that pop up on this screen are hyperlinks, URL addresses that can be clicked on to bring you directly to the site.

If the keywords typed in do not provide helpful results, try other words. After all, a search engine's keywords are only as creative as the people who design web pages. When site developers, or creators, develop a site, they provide a list of keywords and terms that can be used on search engines to bring users to their sites.

◀ *Google.com is such a popular search engine that "to google" has worked its way into our vocabulary.*

Sized to Fit

File compression squeezes a computer file down to its smallest possible size. Smaller files take up less computer memory when stored and can travel over the Internet faster.

Compressing a file usually involves the use of a special software program that replaces frequently occurring words or data with smaller symbols. Those smaller symbols expand back into full words or data when the file is decompressed. If a computer user sends a compressed file to another computer, the receiver should be able to download the file—save it from the Internet onto his or her computer—and then open it decompressed, if his or her computer has a compression program. When a computer cannot decompress a file, it will display an error message or allow the user to open a file filled with meaningless symbols and stray words.

▲ *A compressed file appears as meaningless symbols.*

MISTAKEN IDENTITY

What if a web server cannot understand a request for a file?

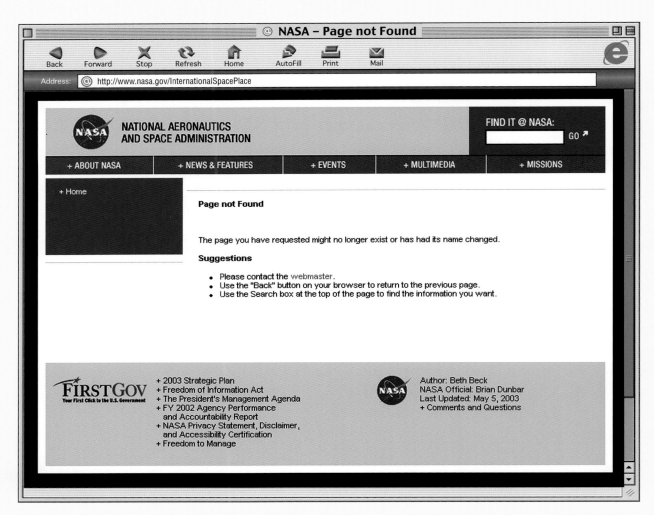

It sends an error message back to the user. One tiny mistake in typing the URL address—such as a missing period, or a forward slash instead of a backslash —will put a quick stop to any surfing.

A request for an incorrect address will sprint from router to router just like any other request. If the request names a domain that does not exist, your computer will soon give up—because it will receive no response to its request. On the other hand, if the domain is correct, the request will reach the server, but the bad URL will return the wrong file, or no file at all.

For example, if you are looking for information on the International Space Station and type in *http://www.nasa.gov/InternationalSpacePlace/*, routers will direct the request to NASA's website because the first half of the address is correct. However, once the request is directed to NASA's computer server, NASA's server will figure out that there is no "InternationalSpacePlace" directory.

When the server recognizes an incorrect URL address, it will send a message back saying that the information provided was incorrect.

A World of Their Own

While the Internet is meant for worldwide use, many businesses operate smaller versions to serve the needs of their company. Intranets are private, password-protected computer networks set up by businesses to simplify interoffice e-mailing, group scheduling, and access to company databases and essential files.

Intranets use TCP/IP networks and offer access to the World Wide Web and e-mail, among other Internet tools. However, intranets are separated from the Internet and outside computer users by a firewall, a mix of hardware and software that blocks outsiders, to protect company information. Intranet e-mail and data retrieval work the same as they would on the Internet, but users' requests must pass through the firewall first.

▼ *Companies may create private, secure networks for internal use.*

ISP Puts Website On-Line

How did the website get on the server's computer network in the first place?

Websites get put on the Internet the same way users do: through Internet service providers (ISPs). Therefore, both computer users and site developers need to register with an ISP to get to "work," in the form of Internet access. Without a connection to a server, producers of websites would have no link to the World Wide Web and its audience.

But how do the producers actually put their website on the ISP's server?

Even Computers Need NAPs

An ISP is needed to use the Internet and get a website on the Internet, but getting the world's ISPs to work together is a whole other concern. A Network Access Point (NAP) is a computer network exchange facility where ISPs from around the world can connect with one another in peering arrangements. Peering means that the ISPs agree to send data packets across certain system routers, in order to keep all data moving quickly on the Internet.

Small or mid-sized ISPs can make peering arrangements with each other, but most major providers have their own NAPs with ready-made connections that determine how traffic will be routed. Not surprisingly, these connection points are where most Internet traffic occurs as computer user requests pass through constantly.

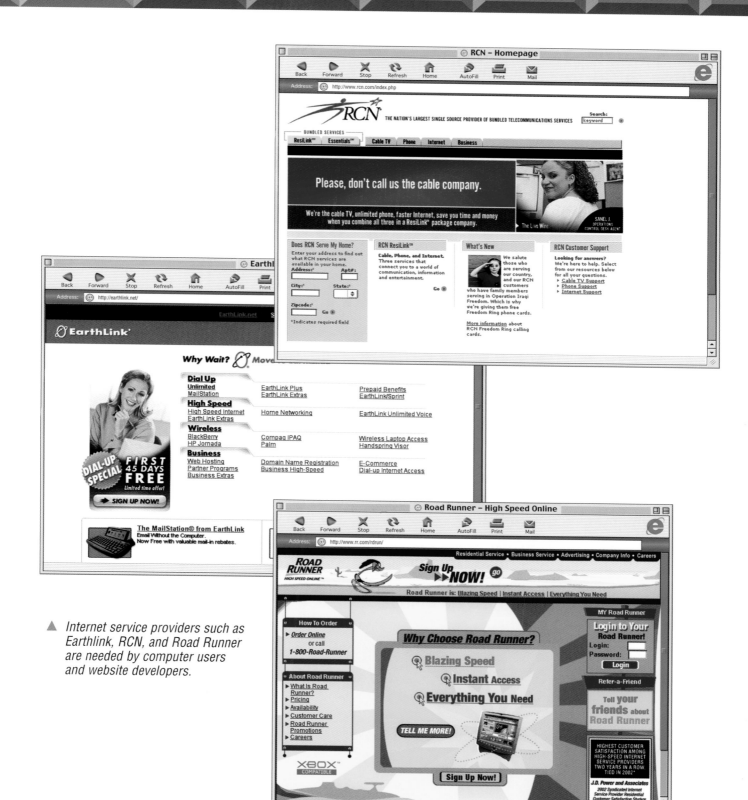

▲ Internet service providers such as Earthlink, RCN, and Road Runner are needed by computer users and website developers.

Developers Add Site Files to Server

How do the developers actually put their website on the ISP's server?

They use the File Transfer Protocol (FTP). An FTP program allows the developer (or anyone with the proper username and password) to upload, or add, pages to the server, and make changes to the website.

Before a site can be put on the server, the developers must register to receive a domain name (for example, nasa.gov) so the site will have a unique URL address. This can often be done through the ISP.

By this time, the site may already be designed. That means graphics and words are in place and the images are in a format that a computer can understand.

What is needed for a computer to understand an image?

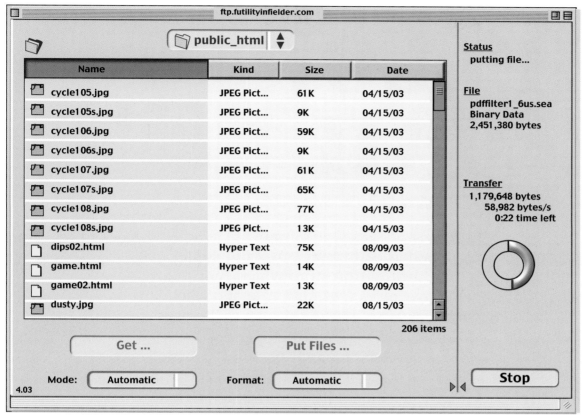

Name	Kind	Size	Date
cycle105.jpg	JPEG Pict...	61K	04/15/03
cycle105s.jpg	JPEG Pict...	9K	04/15/03
cycle106.jpg	JPEG Pict...	59K	04/15/03
cycle106s.jpg	JPEG Pict...	9K	04/15/03
cycle107.jpg	JPEG Pict...	61K	04/15/03
cycle107s.jpg	JPEG Pict...	65K	04/15/03
cycle108.jpg	JPEG Pict...	77K	04/15/03
cycle108s.jpg	JPEG Pict...	13K	04/15/03
dips02.html	Hyper Text	75K	08/09/03
game.html	Hyper Text	14K	08/09/03
game02.html	Hyper Text	13K	08/09/03
dusty.jpg	JPEG Pict...	22K	08/15/03

ftp.futilityinfielder.com — public_html

Status putting file...

File pdffilter1_6us.sea Binary Data 2,451,380 bytes

Transfer 1,179,648 bytes 58,982 bytes/s 0:22 time left

206 items

Get ...   Put Files ...

Mode: Automatic   Format: Automatic   Stop

4.03

▲ *A directory shows all the components of a website, ready for delivery to an ISP using File Transfer Protocol.*

Personal Space

To receive a domain name, producers must register their sites with a domain name registrar. This process is run by the Internet Corporation for Assigned Names and Numbers, which certifies ISPs and other companies as domain name registrars. Registrars charge for registering a domain name, and request a yearly fee. Only they are allowed to access and modify an international master database of domain names.

If a producer wants to create a domain name, he or she should first check a "whois" server (one collection can be found at *www.allwhois.com*) that keeps a list of all the registered domain names. Just as two people can have the same phone number with a different area code, however, producers can be given the same URL address with different domain endings. In other words, *www.nasa.gov* and *www.nasa.org* can both exist, but they are different websites created by different producers, carrying different information.

▲ *A website for registering a domain name*

HELLO, E-MAIL

How does e-mail work?

Electronic mail, or e-mail, addresses provide computer users with a destination from which they can send and receive text messages and attached files. Internet service providers have computer users who register with them and pay a fee to reach the Internet through their computer server. The addresses are given out by ISPs or a local server, such as a business or organization with its own server. To be sure that no two people in the world have the same e-mail address, each ISP and server keeps track of its e-mail addresses.

A typical e-mail address would look like this: *TessH@myemailserver.com*. The user creates the first part of an e-mail address, called a name or screen name ("TessH" in this case). Users can choose almost any series of letters or numbers as a screen name. TessH's ISP or computer server determines the second part of the address. The "at" sign (@) separates the two pieces of information to show a link. For example, the address TessH@myemailserver.com could belong to a computer user named "TessH" at a server called "myemailserver."

Sorry, That Line Is Busy

If you have ever tried to get your e-mail and been suddenly disconnected or gotten a busy signal, you know that the high-speed world of Internet information travel can come to a halt for the same reason cars stop on the highway: traffic.

The millions of computers that offer Internet information are matched and sometimes exceeded by the number of computer users who are trying to access that information at the same time. That is why e-mail users may get a busy signal when connecting online, why some search requests take longer than others do, and why a connection may quit while the computer user is surfing. Times when traffic is heavy differ in each part of the world because time zones are different. But user beware: Lunchtime is often the busiest.

▲ *When this symbol appears on your screen, your computer may be stalled getting on-line by Internet traffic.*

BEHIND THE 'NET

How does a developer know the website is ready to be viewed by Internet users?

Once developers have a domain name, they can upload, or place, their site on a server. Through the server, they can view their site on the "hidden" Internet. By typing in a URL address, developers can preview their site to see if it looks and reads the way they planned and is user-friendly. This gives the developer a chance to make changes to the site before anyone else sees it.

The site is technically on the web in this stage. To keep other surfers out, though, the ISP provides a pop-up screen requesting the developer's username and password before the page can be viewed.

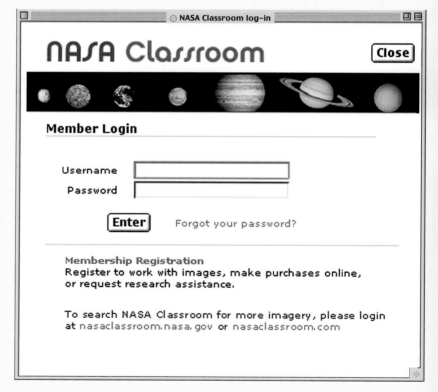

Making the Customer Happy

Besides checking the text and pictures, developers do the following to be sure their site is ready for the public.

1. Click on hyperlinks to be sure users are directed to the intended destinations.

2. Try the site at different transfer speeds to test how long it takes for the web pages to appear on computers that process information at different speeds. While most computers now have modems that transfer information at 56 kbps (kilobites per second), older computers may have slower modems. If a page has large files, transfer time may take too long.

3. View the site using different browsers and computer models, which may translate site files differently.

4. View the site in varying resolutions—the amount of on-screen sharpness and clarity—to be sure the design of each page is not ruined.

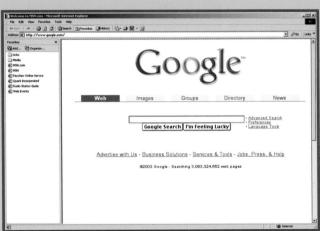

▲ *Four different browsers display the Google home page.*

Images Formatted for Internet Use

What is needed for a computer to understand an image?

Images must be in a special format that a computer can understand so that they can be seen on screen and moved or changed by the producers. The most popular image formats are Graphics Interchange Format (GIF) and Joint Photographic Experts Group (JPEG).

GIF images are limited to 256 colors and used for logos, banners, and computer-generated art. JPEGs can have millions of colors and are usually used for photographs and other large, detailed images. Both of these formats work with the help of image editing programs, such as Paint Shop Pro. Such programs change images like a photograph or a printed piece of art into these image formats, and then give producers the tools to make each one the size, color, and shape they want.

How are printed images translated into image formats?

GIF images are limited in colors and are generally used for logos or displays. ▶

▲ JPEG images are used for photos and large, detailed images.

▲ Image editing programs allow a producer to link small pictures with larger versions.

Different Strokes

Image editing programs do a lot more than just make a page look nice. They provide the developer with some of the tools needed to make the site user-friendly. For example, they can help reduce the size of an image, which will decrease the file size of an image—that, in turn, makes the image appear on the user's screen faster as the website opens.

These editing programs also allow the producer to link thumbnail-sized pictures with a larger version of the same image. This way, computer users can quickly look at the thumbnails, click on a picture, and have the larger version pop up on their screen. This saves time and computer memory.

Printed Images are Scanned and Stored as a Separate File

How are printed images translated into image formats?

All noncomputer-generated images must be scanned before they can be used as JPEGs or GIFs. To scan an image, the producer must place a printed version of the image in a scanner, a device that reads words and illustrations on paper and translates the information into a format computers can use. The scanner then digitizes the image, organizing it into a grid of boxes called pixels with predetermined codes inside each one. This creates a computer-ized version of the image.

The computer scan then can be stored on a computer as a separate file. This file can be translated into an image format, and redesigned on-screen with an editing program to fit the producer's needs.

Where the image will go on a web page has usually been decided before the image is edited.

How is placement of images communicated?

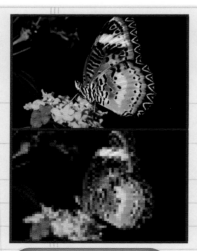

Dots to Dots

Images can be scanned in different ways. If the final result, shown on the computer screen, is sharp and detailed, the image was scanned at a high resolution. Images with less detail and clarity were scanned at a lower resolution. High resolution images may look better, but they also take up a lot of memory and are slower to download than low resolution images.

Resolution is measured by how densely the image shows up on the computer screen. The higher the resolution of the scanned image, the more pixels it uses per square inch of the computer screen. Resolution quality is noted by the term "pixels per inch," or "ppi." Another notation, also used for printers, is "dots per inch," or "dpi."

◄ *The top image has been scanned at a higher resolution than the bottom one.*

▲ *A photograph of a sunflower is ready to be scanned*

Site Is Coded with HTML

How is placement of images communicated?

The entire design of a website—layout, images, and text—is actually coded in a single HTML file that is stored in the computer and accessible from the server.

An HTML file is a text document that can be typed in on any computer word-processing program. The document itself consists of the page's text and HTML-coded instructions, called tags, that describe how the page should look. The tags are contained in angle brackets (< >).

Usually, opening and closing tags surround each piece of text that receives special treatment—in terms of style, color, or size—on the site. Closing tags contain slashes (/).

HTML is like any other foreign language—hard to understand, unless you study it. At right are some commonly used tags.

But how do producers decide what images and pictures to put on their site?

News Flash

One of the most eye-catching ways to spice up a web page is to include special extras, such as Flash and Shockwave files. These file formats offer animated images or text that can grab a computer user's attention.

The problem with these tools is that not every computer can use them. Using Flash and Shockwave players requires plug-ins, software tools that add a specific feature or service to a browser. The plug-ins are generally available free on the web to computer users who want them—for example, Shockwave and Flash plug-ins are available on creator Macromedia's site (*www.macromedia.com/software*). A computer must, however, have a good deal of memory to handle these fancy features.

Source of http://nasaclassroom.nasa.gov/kidsinspace/solar.html

```html
<html>
    <head>
        <title>Kids In Space: The Solar System</title>
    </head>
    <body BGCOLOR="#000033" TEXT="#FFFFFF" LINK="#66FFFF" VLINK="#33FF33" ALINK="#FF0000">
        <h1 ALIGN="center">The Solar System</h1>
        <p ALIGN="center"><img SRC="HTTP://STARCHILD.GSFC.NASA.GOV/Images/heasarc/icons/shut_l.gif"
alt="Shuttle"></p>
        <p>
            <img BORDER=0 ALT="The Solar System"
SRC="HTTP://STARCHILD.GSFC.NASA.GOV/Images/StarChild/solar_system_level2/solar_system_small.gif" ALIGN=RIGHT
HSPACE=25>
            The words &quot;<a HREF ="solar_system.html">solar system</a>&quot; refer to the Sun
and all of the objects that travel around it. These objects include planets, natural <a HREF ="satellite.html
">satellites</a> such as the Moon, the <a HREF ="asteroid.html">asteroid</a> belt, <a HREF
="comet.html">comets</a>, and <a HREF ="meteoroid.html">meteoroids</a>. Our solar system has an <a HREF
="elliptical.html">elliptical</a> shape and is part of a <a HREF ="galaxy.html">galaxy</a> known as the Milky
Way. The Sun is the center of the solar system. It contains 99.8% of all of the <a HREF="mass.html">mass</a> in
our solar system. Consequently, it exerts a tremendous <a HREF="gravitational_pull.html">gravitational pull</a>
on planets, satellites, asteroids, comets, and meteoroids. <a HREF="astronomer.html"> Astronomers</a> believe
the solar system formed 4.5 billion years ago. However, they differ in their beliefs about how the system
formed. Some believe the whole solar system formed from a single flat cloud of gas, while others believe it
formed when a huge object passed near the Sun, pulling a stream of gas off of the Sun. Astronomers theorize the
planets then formed from this gas stream.
        </p>
        <br><br><br>
        <center>
            <table CELLPADDING=5 CELLSPACING=5 BORDER=5>
                <tr>
                    <td><a HREF="sun.html">The Sun</a><br></td>
                    <td><a HREF="planets.html">The Planets</a><br></td>
                </tr>
                <tr>
                    <td><a HREF="moon.html">The Moon</a><br></td>
                    <td><a HREF="asteroids.html">Asteroids</a><br></td>
                </tr>
                <tr>
                    <td><a HREF="meteoroids.html">Meteoroids</a><br></td>
                    <td><a HREF="comets.html">Comets</a><br></td>
                </tr>
            </table>
        </center>
    </body>
</html>
```

HTML	Identifies the document as an HTML document
HEAD	Contains information about a web page's heading
BODY	Notes the main content of a web page
CENTER	Centers text
P	Starts a new paragraph
BR	Starts a new line of text
CAPTION	Creates a caption, or sentence, under an image
IMG	Adds an image

A single HTML file (top) contains all the words and pictures in a website (bottom).

Producers Plan a Site

How do producers decide what will be on a web page?

It depends on their needs and who is sponsoring, or paying for, the site. There are many reasons why people and groups create a website. Businesses may make one to reach customers. An organization may create a site to promote its ideas or provide information. Individuals may find that it is an easy way to share information about themselves or their interests with the rest of the world. Once people decide they want a site, they can either produce their own site or hire producers to do it for them.

After producers create concepts, figure out their audience and its needs, and decide how they want to present information, they analyze how what they want to express can be portrayed on the web. Their site planning usually begins with the home page, which commonly offers information on what the site is about, what it offers, and who sponsors it. Also important to the site's creators are the hyperlinks that let visitors move around the site and visit other pages with related information. With a little luck, someday someone just might surf the Internet and visit their site!

A lot of planning goes into ► the creation of a website.

DIO78H9L8QBGMSGREUMDOVL18IWMB0ELL4UKNGNER2B2F9EIN2IF92YV4ASDMUK7PPFUAHX70KYGZ6XH
GH0DADTMPQM9V8EV335R0HRFQKUWK22S7PP K J3AT XFGB98PZL2UJHFID14DICAR6L78YJR562B
EY02HLCF0APD2EGC4DDJCUJLWXFOA TR6QWP4XCFJ2E6MP1ID25K01HOZB5CKFC
VDNWBPW3J7J0IJLXF6G1QI3D1K AWTUYSEE3456LJIN45ELC7LOGGEJHKQ
B1ZXL05FT7AX0I8E680BLL0VM 5IM31DDFW11RWW2B5VNQHTN2035IY
HIJLL1PHTLX8A8877UYL1HLV T6EVNO4NFK1EY8W5MRJ481C4JB0C
BGPI10ZVR8XT40TTP4A8VWRY HK OLCPY8G712DA43X8Y6KE1N86CF7J
FAP40JMIM0LL22D3CAM21K1KD P ANS7EB07CPD42474XLMKY4DHQ4G1
55VQ2ZX8ZYTEAU78PC8R1C6M M 04M62X K63I LC 8GPBKTC9M9DKNECT8A0I7AFF8V0J
WFPWIMUN2TP3PKBC1CT296UP 3 I00LYKH MQWV34WY 5R D5803894HVYD2RIMEHHJVYQWY133
VKAQYK08639VBK2P2N0IH1Q5WM JA9UQ1KK L33BN3R1 090WPMU42LDWV6B47PJCH08UWVO5LBT
RKFT2M5GQ267EE2W0G3QIBQ8 T78DEY C1 CD3VG3 HRIBN2B1KN5VALJEBP5Q5NEBKCUP
WDNQY2MOHX765KKMXWXM8VHK J00 9VQGG2RE5PUW85YALK0O3HMRCGZ9
X4VI0QL0V2 LYJWANTJFMJBP2Q15GE HXJC CUE HP131ZJR1KD4HODI98V781KCSWN6AM
4X0I2HN3X MQB6G0ZJ0MMKK F K4A 6IS NOR38PDKWFRLI8577M 1P42YEMNW
K8C59HLI J2KJI51VFX3FKUC WDVA FE 4TM5C4PWD5NBVOLW4MP 39690U2J8
8IC0LCI B0C 66I4R2ID6DDYM3T AC8 0 8 G IE 4VD2XRLD8NKYHX9N0I L Q62O4CVO
H5SYL5H C E GFXR8ATZAR8H DXWPO9VRI2Y2DTC R8797P86LHYNCJH 6LK68X2P
EY0GJL38KUYC A H502FMUB7L JPAKKER 4M QNPFLUVF0AYC4 R3LY95H5YDH
8072Z6JIRBUK5KS D9Y80HZK1 GAQB8PP4F5 CH6VCN0UXDPK5Q0J
Q68FVJUFKX5MJCNOU F P00SAGFO JLGH8V9GG3 VVQT6ICH01JP53TIZN2Y
7THVGXVM1IMMNU3B8CFC XL56YX794JG68JYTLTI8IQ YTLN8IE80XLMR7SH4BBIPB5
CBFVWKYB10T85T0LDLP0UTP M25QKPRC4X9GT38 VW50JHZ2J0XVLB88BJJAWNDD2UI
MTAQPB8A8P7CHUVKM30FQVPVI1 0OTMHRZF 5A9TRXTU9W3L71MQ166CDNQY64DG9Z0
AF0MJWUGZ8I08NIXVFUBYN49P38125 N17S3 B2RRFNR9B9E4Q8P714628L14JBDXCMPQK4
MEA118T8GBTKVV3KLPE2ONV8EUJ7F50LFHT Y3KEUAMFCKF0NO6MB6XYDP91YLWTEF7VAH9E8
VXW1LKE5KWHH63KJLKKBGORMCM9M SRRQ OCCLRBPVGRQDF0T9ZPHHNEQ905DM90DMG
XVCNR6M8CY1TDC70V89608N7M MCEGR2LPXTL 26UGUB03XTRR93AL1PPLIADN90C2Y
XQ88ZHHU7B4YDOQ6EQY YN5JU307A4J69T0NTUPE9 GV9XI08MYQF140NGHI6C32MJ
VQBTXA399 CW5 AU1ALZMBTTVQ3MOF448JZ5M2PUT6 6PK4U8RBFQ3LC
JW7DELAXR2 XD6PLPNDQQTAKDI1J0VNFH08G2DD07BBH5AL4UINXM 00 5J91J9P6U9N800UY
VCKBI20WWM9 W H1HW40D1UHF26VKIR6XCSJXT3973L40OH8HA80KGE07 0DBJ6KZ8T9TJERV9D
N6YHR69ZHEE9 6FRMBBQBU75NXGW9CJ0KF7XCQM9D5V0PIX8GC80HEFVV3C YRYXL3RK2BB0V40WQM
CV3NRQXFK95XW2638F828Z8QRDWVCXPP0MJ779X1H79ND9MRW8DX781L6X5C0A8BMGM8PAHURUY36NVP110Z
5WABCC3P2DAKE8Q2FEA0VL8891CRREOUXEGKQFUC3C2O8EX2L3Q8JJ2C4KFP5FC8JXRE7C3BF8Z8Q4YS

Vile Files

All the sharing of files around the Internet can make computer viruses a big headache. Viruses are programs that, once they are loaded onto a computer, can run and copy themselves. Viruses often ruin other files on a normally "healthy" computer and use up the computer's memory. If a computer has a virus, it may spread the problem to other computers when it shares files with them.

All computer viruses are created by humans, and other people have created cures. Since 1987, when a virus infected ARPAnet, the large network used by the U.S. Defense Department and many universities, numerous antivirus programs have been developed. These programs check computer systems for common types of viruses.

The Big Picture

⑫ Web Page Appears on Computer Screen

A web page shows up on the computer of someone connected to the Internet.
(pages 6–7)

⑩ Browser Reassembles Data from Chunks Called Packets

Following codes and instructions called Transmission Control Protocol (TCP), the browser has put chunks of data called packets together into a readable page.
(pages 10–11)

⑦ Servers Pull Correct File According to URL Address

Servers use every piece of a URL address to locate the right file from the right computer server.
(pages 18–19)

⑪ ISP's Server Delivers Web Page, Browser Displays It

The page has been delivered to the computer by the server of the Internet service provider (ISP). The user computer's browser displays it.
(pages 8–9)

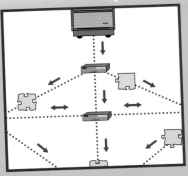

⑨ Protocols Direct Data Transmission and Reassembly

TCP and Internet Protocol (IP) work together to direct reassembly of data and to send it from server to server.
(pages 12–13)

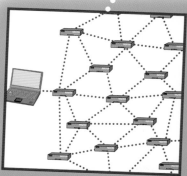

⑧ Routers Deliver Packets to Servers

Routers carry the packets to the networks of computers across the Internet.
(pages 16–17)

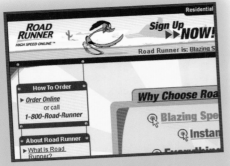

6 Website Is Put On-Line by ISP

The websites have been created by producers and registered with an ISP to get on-line, and onto the ISP's server.
(pages 24–25)

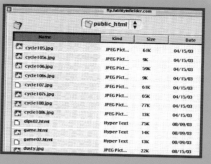

5 Producers Upload Pages to the Server

After registering a domain name, producers use FTP (File Transfer Protocol) to deliver their pages to their server.
(pages 26–27)

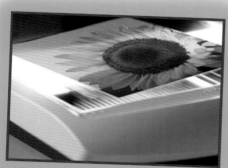

3 Printed Images Are Scanned

A scanner reads images and converts them to a computerized code.
(pages 34–35)

4 Images Are Formatted for the Internet

Images are placed on a web page in JPEG or GIF formats so they can be edited and moved on the computer screen.
(pages 32–33)

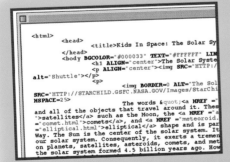

2 Site Is Coded with HTML

HTML directions help the computer place the images on the site. HTML is also used to create and format text on a website.
(pages 36–37)

1 Producers Plan a Site

Web producers plan a website based on audience needs and their own goals.
(pages 38–39)

Internet Database

Symbol Playing

One problem of computer communication is how hard it is to show emotion online. For some e-mail users, the simple exclamation point just is not enough! For that reason—and for fun—they have a number of symbols, called emoticons or smileys, and abbreviations to quickly make a point. Tilt your head to the left to view the emoticon examples.

EMOTICONS	
:-)	*Funny/Happy*
:-(	*Sad*
;-)	*Wink*
:-<<	*Very sad*
%-(	*Angry*
:-/	*Questioning/Confused*
:D	*Laughing out loud*
:O	*Shout*
:'(	*Crying*

ABBREVIATIONS	
ASAP	*As soon as possible*
AFK	*Away from keyboard*
B4	*Before*
BAK	*Back at keyboard*
BTW	*By the way*
CUL8R	*See you later*
G2G	*Got to go*
HTH	*Hope this helps*
IC	*I see*
IDK	*I do not know*
IM	*Instant message*
J/K	*Just kidding*
LOL	*Laughing out loud*
ROTFL	*Rolling on the floor laughing*
TAFN	*That's all for now*
TIA	*Thanks in advance*

Wild, Wild Web

According to a survey conducted by a software manufacturer in April, 2003, there are at least 40 million websites in active use. That is eight times as many sites as were reported in 1999.

Do You Know the Way to .uk?

Here are just a few of the over 240 top-level domains assigned to specific countries. Can you figure out the country to which each domain belongs?

Answers on page 45.

.at	.it
.au	.jp
.br	.mx
.ca	.nz
.de	.pl
.do	.th
.es	.tv
.ie	.uk
.il	.us
.in	.ws
.is	.za

Watch and Learn

Almost 10 percent of the world now has access to the Internet. According to one study, Europe has the highest number of Internet users in the world: about 186 million people. The U.S. and Canada are right behind with about 183 million. The Asia/Pacific region has about 168 million Internet users.

Which websites are visited most by these millions and millions of users? Just like television, the Internet has companies that track user viewing habits for research purposes and to help advertisers find their audiences. These tracking companies analyze data from service providers, site producers, and others to gather information such as how many users are going on-line, what sites people are visiting, and trends in viewers' habits (like the popularity of visiting religious websites on holidays).

▼ *These numbers from a popular Internet audience measurement service, show age and gender breakdown of visitors to a certain site.*

Audience Profile Panel Type: Home and Work

Target	Composition	Number of Sessions per Month	Average Time Spent During Month	Average Pages Viewed Per Month
Total	100.00	33	18: 44: 56	1215
MALE	49.87	38	21: 48: 22	1438
FEMALE	50.13	29	15: 52: 28	1006
2-11	6.26	5	31: 05: 15	202
12-17	10.29	16	9: 35: 44	580
18-20	3.79	19	11: 08: 07	772
21-24	3.92	34	21: 50: 14	1521
25-34	16.18	40	24: 05: 00	1693

Wonders and Words

Questions & Answers

Q: *Who first used the phrase "Surfing the Internet"?*

A: Many people credit Jean Armour Polly, an American author and former librarian, with first using the term in a June 1992 library bulletin. Still, even Armour Polly admits that, while she came up with the term on her own, she may not have been the first to use it. The term was also used in official e-mails by computer scientists and industry professionals around the same time. Most early users of the term generally relate their use to the fact that looking at web pages is like TV "channel surfing"—moving through various channels, flowing past one to another.

Q: *Are the Internet and World Wide Web the same thing?*

A: They are related, but different. The Internet is a massive network of computer networks that connects millions of computers around the world for communication purposes. The web is a way of accessing information over the Internet—it is basically a tool used on the Internet. The web requires use of browsers to access linked web pages with graphics, sounds, text, and video. E-mail, among other things, is part of the Internet.

Q: *Who named the World Wide Web?*

A: Tim Berners-Lee struggled with a name for the network of computers that could be used by the public to exchange information. He considered Infomesh—information meshed, or mixed, together. Then there was The Information Mine. But Berners-Lee knew the name's acronym would be part of the system, and using the letters TIM would make it appear that he named it after himself.

Finally, the World Wide Web was suggested. Berners-Lee discussed it with his wife, Nancy, and business associates, some of whom noted that it was a bit "stupid" because "www" takes longer to say than "World Wide Web." Still, Berners-Lee was satisfied with it, and the name stuck.

Q: *What is the "@" symbol used for in e-mail addresses?*

A: That symbol, used to separate the local part of an e-mail address from the ISP or server name, is commonly called the "at sign" or a "commercial at," but it also can be called a whorl, snail, or strudel. It is actually a very old symbol, and appears to have first been used in a Roman commercial document signed in 1536, during the Italian Renaissance. There, it stood for the Latin preposition "ad," which meant "at."

Q: *How do the forward and backward arrows on a computer screen know what sites have been viewed?*

A: The arrows are getting that information from the browser. A web browser remembers the last addresses that were typed into the address line, so the next time the user opens the browser, he or she will not have to enter the entire address again. Instead, the user can select it by clicking the arrow behind the address line. Also, the browser keeps track of all the pages visited in one session, so the user can jump back and forth between pages. The pages visited can be stored as history as an option.

Glossary

Browser: Software used to navigate the web, retrieve documents and other files, and display them on a computer user's screen. The most popular browsers are Netscape Navigator and Microsoft Internet Explorer.

Domain Name: An addressing system for websites that includes an organization or server name and a domain suffix (.com, .edu, etc.) The name for NASA's website is "nasa.gov."

File Transfer Protocol (FTP): A protocol, or language, used to send and retrieve files across the Internet.

Hypertext: A formatting process used on the web to link documents by making particular words or phrases "clickable"—thus providing a link to other documents.

HyperText Markup Language (HTML): Shorthand computer language that uses tags, or codes with symbols, as instructions for a browser on how a website should look.

HyperText Transfer Protocol (HTTP): A protocol, or language, used to send and retrieve files across the Internet.

Internet: The massive, international network of linked computer networks.

Packet: Pieces of coded information that can be sent over a computer network by routers.

Protocol: A common format that all computers understand in order to exchange files.

Router: A systematic tool used to quickly and efficiently direct packets of information between different computer networks.

Server: Any computer connected to a network, but usually used to describe those from which information (such as a web page) is taken. Also called "host."

Transmission Control Protocol/Internet Protocol (TCP/IP): This protocol system, which made the Internet possible, works to analyze information and create packets of information to send them to computers around the world.

Uniform Resource Locator (URL): The address of a document that includes the specific protocol, server domain name, and the file location. For example, "http://www.nasa.gov/ntv/" specifies using the HTTP protocol (others include FTP or GOPHER), on the server, and the directory "ntv."

World Wide Web (WWW): A protocol, or tool, used to access information on the Internet.

Answers (page 43)

.at	Austria	**.do**	Dominican Republic	**.it**	Italy	**.tv**	Tuvalu
.au	Australia	**.es**	Spain	**.jp**	Japan	**.uk**	United Kingdom
.br	Brazil	**.ie**	Ireland	**.mx**	Mexico	**.us**	United States
.ca	Canada	**.il**	Israel	**.nz**	New Zealand	**.ws**	Western Samoa
.de	Germany	**.in**	India	**.pl**	Poland	**.za**	South Africa
		.is	Iceland	**.th**	Thailand		

Index

Credits

Credits:

Produced by: J.A. Ball Associates, Inc.
Jacqueline Ball, Justine Ciovacco, Andrew Willett
Daniel H. Franck, Ph.D., Science Consultant

Art Direction, Design, and Production:
designlabnyc
Todd Cooper, Sonia Gauba, Jay Jaffe

Writer: Justine Ciovacco

Cover: Brooke Fasani: boy using computer; Ablestock/Hemera: modem; Jay Jaffe: browser window; Andrew Willett: html code; Corbis: web server.

Interior: Brooke Fasani: p.7 boy using computer, pp.28–29 girl using keyboard, boy and girl creating web page; Ablestock/Hemera: p.2 computer, p.7 computer, mouse, modem, p.10 modem, p.11 monitor, p.23 network hub, p.33 web page, p.34 butterfly, p.35 scanner, pp.40–41 background; Todd Cooper: p.8 online ads, pp.14–15, 16–17 diagrams; courtesy of NASA: p.9 web page, p.11 web page, p.13 diagram, p.19 web page, p.22 web page, Jay Jaffe: p.12 other protocols, p.15 camouflage computer chip, p.27 directory for FutilityInfielder.com, p.30 web page; ArtToday: p.14 Tim Berners-Lee, p.29 watch icon, pp.32–33 gif and jpg images,; PhotoDisc, Inc: p.17 satellite, p.42 computer chip, pp.44–45, 48 backgrounds; courtesy of Google™: pp.20, 31 web pages; courtesy of RCN: p.25 web page; courtesy of Earthlink: p.22 web page; courtesy of AOL/Time Warner™: p.22 web page; courtesy of Verisign™: p.27 web page; Andrew Willett: p.21 meaningless symbols, p.37 source code, web page, p.39 digital skull and cross bones; Sonia "Web-Jockey" Gauba: p.42, 43 web pages

For More Information

Eddings, Joshua. *How the Internet Works. New York: Ziff-Davis Press, 1994.*

Gralla, Preston. *How the Internet Works: Millennium Edition. New York: Que/Macmillan Computer Publishing, 1999.*

www.internettrafficreport.com
This site gives a report, updated every five minutes, on how fast data is moving across different zones of the Internet around the world.

www.livinginternet.com
This site gives comprehensive information about how the Internet (and the technologies that use the Internet) works.

www.pbs.org/opb/nerds2.0.1/
This site is a companion to the PBS television series **Nerds 2.0.1.** It gives a history of the Internet, explanations of the technology that runs it, and biographies of the people who helped create it.

www.webopedia.com
This site gives definitions of computer and Internet-related terms.